THE
SUMMER
KING

POEMS JOANNA PRESTON

The Summer King

OTAGO
UNIVERSITY
PRESS

The Summer King was
the inaugural winner of
The Kathleen Grattan Award
for a collection of poetry, 2008.

Published by Otago University Press
Level 1, 398 Cumberland Street
PO Box 56, Dunedin, New Zealand
E: university.press@otago.ac.nz
F: 64 9 479 8385
W: www.otago.ac.nz/press

First published 2009
Copyright © Joanna Preston 2009
ISBN 978 1 877372 69 8

Design by Sarah Maxey
Printed through Condor Production Ltd,
Hong Kong

For my grandmother, Mary Harris,
who always said this would happen,
and Stewart Collie, who makes it possible

Contents

The Summer King

Before the boar stops twitching
Dad and Jeff slash his throat.
Blood on autumn grass –
a torrent of curses
gush from his new-made mouth.

The iron bathtub broods in the flames,
its belly of water ripening.
We slide the boar in,
glide the razor's bright tongue
across his skin.

Pale flag, he hangs
by his heels from the gambrel.
Dad slits him open, balls to neck
and omens spill out
in dark coils of gut.

The hand that feeds,
the bullet, the knife –
I am learning their language.

In the Voices of Tarapunga
(for Judith)

'I dreamed we were at the Heads,
scattered across the face of the cliff,
all of us who'd loved her, me clinging
to tussock just under the rim.
The wind sent fingers plucking at my clothes,
and the damned moon still
had its back turned. Starlight
edged every wave with steel.

She came back. Walked
barefoot out of the sea.
Everyone stretched out their hands,
calling to her
in the voices of tarapunga.
But she rose up past them
until she was level with me.
She reached out her broken hand,
said something I couldn't hear.
Then she stepped up onto the headland
and into the air.'

Lighthouse Keeper

I've strewn kelp and sea lettuce over the metal stairs
– she'll like that. Even the walls smell of her.

When night spreads to extinguish the land
I put this lighthouse to her work,

pick out fishing boats and container ships
infesting the sea like lice in a seal's pelt.

I send them onto the rocks, vessels filled
with the cold weight of my devotion.

Afterwards, she sings to me
in a voice so high I can barely hear.

She left me a gift once – a femur
studded with barnacles where her lips had rested.

I lean from the railing and imagine letting go,
feel my body smash a path through the thick air

I've almost forgotten the point of a day-lit sky.
I wake at sunset drenched, and sticky with the salt
        taste of her.

Skeleton

To hurl your own bones
skull first
down a twisting
chine of ice,

on a dinner tray
balanced
on two steel blades

this
is free-fall,
air banked
like snow

rime on the lip
of high, sharp bends,
teeth an inch
from the ice

speed is bled
into frozen walls,
skin shaking rush
toe-steered,

body straight
a falcon's stoop

the thin pane
of fontanelle,

a pulse, to be
unborn again

but ready this time,
headfirst
and down

into the cold,
the brilliant
light.

Song of Wire
after Anthony Lawrence

I broke free once
went for the fencer
like a tiger snake

slashed his thigh
to the bone
taught him to sing.

I have tasted
the iron tang
of blood

now I watch
you.

Hear me
crooning
to the easterly

whetting
my single
silver tooth

whispering insurrection
to the strainer post.

The Valley Farmers

This is the slow unfolding of night,
the road homewards in thickening shadow,
a spill of light glinting like copper wire
as the sun slips from the last smudge of cloud.

Farm-wives will be calling their ducks,
feeding the dogs, setting flame to kindling
before closing their doors on dusk.
There will be meat, and bread, and ease
for tired men with soil in their skin.

And then night: the last light doused,
pale bodies unclothed, and a low bed
where we too can unmake ourselves.

Cowarral

i Daybreak

From my bed on the back verandah
white-stippled paddocks reach
all the way to the mountains.
Frost has etched the lines
of cobwebs into the brittle air.

The sway-backed mare drowses
surrounded by wraiths of breath,
each long eyelash tipped
with a bead of moisture –
its own sliver of sun.

A kookaburra scrapes his beak
along the low branch
of the old persimmon. Soon
he will throttle the stillness,
and thaw this silver morning.

ii The Orange Tree

Older than all of us, dowry for a new life.
A sapling rough-swaddled in hessian,
dragged behind a bullock dray
across rivers named as they went.

It kept want at bay – at leaf-tip, root-tip.
Fruit against the leaves was the glow
of campfires seen from a mountain pass.
It anchored light to the world.

Satinbirds wove altars to it, offering pieces
of the sky. I disturbed a shield bug
and gave my eyes –

there was pain, and three days
of blindness, as though I'd looked
into the face of a god.

iii **A Summer Storm**

At first light the sky tore open.
I padded barefoot through a maze of boxes
to close all the windows.
I opened the curtains and curled up on the sill

as I used to curl up on Great Grandma's lap
to watch storms sweep down
from the mountain

named for a man
she'd been widow to most of her life.

From the ark of her armchair
we'd spell our names between thunder
that rattled the china and knocked out the power.

mist on the mountain means rain on the way

Light grew rich and heavy
until the horses blazed like molten bronze.
Once, lightning blasted a mountain oak
halfway up the red-clay ridge,

sent shrapnel of timber out eighty feet.
The stump burned through two nights of rain –
I could see the glow from my bed.

Rain falls almost silent against a slate roof,
and two panes of glass keep weather at a distance.
Those storms roared on corrugated iron,
and ended the world at verandah's edge.

But when I went out and stood
on the lawn in my nightshirt, mud
welling around the pale of my feet,
I offered my face to the English rain

and she was behind me,
one hand resting on the verandah post,
waiting for me
to close my eyes, to step back.

iv **Homecoming**

First is the sign and the turn-off,
the slowing of the car, the unsealed road – and now
you are coming home.

Window down, driving up the valley
past silky oaks and willows
and the night-song of frogs.

Remember how the old persimmon
frames the sunrise?

How the river offers its welcome
in a language you have forgotten?

The Inlet Bridge rattles its name as you cross.
Moonlight bleaches the lucerne paddocks
and deepens the shadows.

But the gate at the top of the lane
is propped open. You stop.
There's no light from the house.

v Bede's Sparrow

Four huge tree trunks anchored us here.
A flood that took the tractor
could only silt the carpets.
Old house, full of our ghosts.

Now they've stripped the tin from the roof,
the hearth, the chimney that soared like a spire
past sides of bacon, curing.
They've ripped out the timbers,
the long, polished boards of the kitchen floor
that I helped Grandma scrub.
They've torn the heavy doors from their hinges

a thousand miles away
I still hear
the exact note they make,
slamming shut.

I wanted to walk just once more
through the wash-house, into the darkness
under the loquat,
to follow the concrete path
that led through the cunjevoi
like a faltering voice.

To step out into sunlight, onto the lawn,
fly like Bede's sparrow
through that one lit room.

Moth

Grey and drab, beating
against your window pane.
Before long
his wings will be tattered streamers
trailing like a thread,
a seam unravelling.

Counting my Blessings

I've never had my hair catch fire
in the middle of preparing dinner, although
sometimes it has been the colour of fire,
and on nor'west days when the static builds,
careless brushing could start a
conflagration.

I've never been stalked by a wolf
through the woods on the way
to my Grandmother's house, although
last time I saw her, the man from next door
stared strangely at me
from his woodheap.

I've never been seduced by a God
in the form of a swan or a shower of light, although
I'm often taken by sunsets.

I've never kept house
for a man with a locked cellar, stocked
with the bodies of all his ex-wives, although
some men I know lock their briefcases,
to stop secrets ambushing their children.

I've never been kidnapped by Berber
tribesmen, who wanted me for the sons
I could give them, or daughters
whose skin would be whiter
than mare's milk.

I have never tasted mare's milk ...

Wai Mei – Not Quite an Elegy

I am here, half-turned
with your name on my lips,

my hip-high summer disciple
who shared my bath, and wrote secrets
in soap on my skin;

we slept head-to-toe on the verandah,
rode bareback through paddocks of bracken.

And, glittering Circe
in starling black for my wedding,
four gold rings in each ear.

You were grown and gone
in the time it took to brush my hair.

The Bat

A kite flown by night-gods,
brittle sticks and parchment,
a fox-eared scrap of skin
whose panic compressed
the cavernous room to the size
of two hands and the flutter
of a heartbeat with teeth exposed
and a scream that I could see

but not hear, a scream
that broke through the doorway
out from under the eaves and tendrils
of snail-vine to the sky and stars
and the sound of the river in moonlight.

Phlogiston

It glowered from its box
growling and hissing,

a beautiful thing, caged
behind a brass screen.

I hugged myself, stared
back at it for hours,

its scent draped
around me like fox-furs.

Dangerous
was just a word

until it escaped one night
and the neighbours came home

to nothing.

The calcined skull
of their yap-dog

crunched under my heel
like frozen grass.

For Marie-Louise

You'll know the photograph I mean,
your mother, young and luminous,
a stray strand of hair, pale like water
bisecting the glow of her cheek.
A private sun.

Your brother is a dimpled papoose on her back,
his bright eyes fixed
on her hands, peeling apples
with the old silver knife
our grandfather brought out from England.

The light is thick with shadows
and corners. And you are there too,
quiet tenant,
the curve in your mother's skirt.

Gloves

Great Grandmother's gloves were kept for funerals,
in tissue paper, limp as something stillborn.

She drew them on slowly, the grey silk
of the other self she wore.

Through each service they lay folded
on her lap, water-stained wings of a moth.

Afterwards, she gives them to me
to put away, still warm, and marked
where her wedding band has worn to gold wire.

She slides the long pins out of her hair,
and I brush until it hangs, a fall
of frozen water down her spine.

She sends me to the garden for fresh flowers
and sits for a while, just visible through the
        open door,
straight-backed and still, with naked hands.

The Bull Sale

One by one the bulls muscle in
like nightclub bouncers –
all balls and beard, or rather
all balls and back-end.

The auctioneer wipes the sweat
from his face. Hands flash
and the bids charge and climb
to clash in the air
above the sawdust and bull shit.

A tight-skinned bull,
scrotum swinging
in the centre of it all – a god
in bull's form, his forehead a thick plate
of bone, hard as a butcher's block.

Photograph from China

This is a photograph of my brother
with his usual half-nervous smirk.
Behind him, the tigers of Lau Hu Tan leap,
teeth bared white in dull marble jaws.
It's the sullen end of winter.
This is before he rode with the Kazakhs.

For the first time, I see that he is tall,
his boots and jacket suit him.
He stands in front of a children's playground
where no one plays, and the paths are spotless.
This is before he tried to visit Tibet.

His chin is gritted with stubble,
his yellow shirt the only bright colour.
The hillside behind him is netted in metal,
a 'bird sanctuary', where people can't go.
This is before he stumbled into North Korea.

And this is before the coffee shop,
before two men grabbed and slapped the girl
and he leapt up like Galahad,
fists cocked, shouting abuse
xun jing! someone hissed, *they're police!*
        and the room stopped.

I can feel the cold wind that ruffles his hair,
for the first time notice his balding scalp.
Behind him, the tigers of Lau Hu Tan leap.
Please - this photograph is of my brother.

Lydia of the Lace Doilies

Of course, she always had hordes of lovers –
so whenever I saw her, fat and placid
termite-queen of the nursing home

I imagined her naked, lying
on a bed of animal fur,
                              small
moustachioed men, smelling
of horses and sweat and woodsmoke

taking turns to lose themselves
in her plump white breasts,
her eyes closed, her full-blown
rose lips
                    parting and unparting.

Light

Uncle Mick swore
he'd seen light spilling
out of the chimney -

bubbles of light
swollen like eggplants
floating across the roof

tumbling over
the guttering
to the clothesline

where Mama's nightie
flapped like a tethered
bird -

a heron perhaps
a pelican with a bill
big enough to swallow

the moon - Auntie Lill
said it was the whiskey
talking.

The Hill Paddock

Searching for the missing calf
in the brittle light of winter afternoon

we found instead
a tuft of bloodied feathers
fluttering in the ryegrass

as though they could remember flight,
and longed for it.

Edge

The gleam of light
from the edge of the cold
curved blade of Grandpa's sickle
hung like a harvested moon
in the darkest corner of the barn.

It followed the tines
of the garden fork,
splayed like his fingers,
probing the vast earth
for constellations
of Kipfler potatoes.

When he died, I saw it leave him,
watched the glaze of shadow
spread, like a bruise
in the lee of his
sharp bones.

Venery

i The Pride of Lions

But before we could marry, he became a lion –
thick pelted, and rich with the musk of beast.

The switch to all fours was not easy – all his weight
slung from the blades of his shoulders.
His deltoids knotted like teak burls,
and I burnished them as he slept.

Burrs matted his mane, and for days
he wouldn't let me groom him –
slapped me away with a suede paw,
snarled against my throat.

He would not eat fruit, or drink milk,
but tore meat from the bones I provided.

His claws caught in the carpet,
so I stripped the rugs from the floor
and polished the boards until they gleamed
and rang with the chime of his nails.

I stroke his saffron hide
and tangle my fingers deep in his ruff,
draw him up around me, ardent
as the gleam of his topaz eyes

– the hypnotic lash of his tail,
the rasp of his tongue on my thighs.

ii A Knot of Toads

We sweated and couldn't sleep.
Darkness purred from a hundred throat-sacs,
a generator left to chug itself to death.

Next morning Aunty's gardening shoes
were sticky-toed and glistening.
They'll fuck anything, Daniel said,
and I learnt a new word
fishing a cane toad out of the pool.

It lay on its back in a puddle,
an old fencing glove brought to life, to hunger
for something I didn't understand.

That night we snuck out in our undies
with a torch to watch them, all
splotchy yellow eyes and warty backs,
climbing each other.

Daniel's skin was smooth, his breath
ragged against my neck.

iii A Husk of Hares

long-footed hare
grazing the contour bank
below the house

arcs of blindness
the black tips of his ears
dance like wagtails

sun just brushing the tips
of the ghost gums
when Jake fetches his rifle

No! shouting *no!*
and cows lift their dark
muzzles as I run

he takes aim

a scream like a child

Christmas morning
dying at my feet

and there is blood
on my night-dress

iv **A Brooding of Hens**

In darkness it scrabbles
at soil and wire netting,
muzzle deep
in the must of my hens.

It bolts as I come running,
a flicker of hunger - gone.

The curled edge of mesh
glints in the torchlight
as I let the dog off her chain.

The hens shuffle, settle again,
a communion of feather and beak.
The bantam in the coop below
tucks her chicks back under;

I cup one in my hands, and listen
to my own dark, feathered heart.

v A Stalk of Foresters

He ran
until he could no longer remember
not running.
His heart was a tocsin
filling his skull, a flood tide
drowning thought.

His axe had fallen long before.
His fingers remembered
the shaft of it, curved
like the throat of a woman,
silken to his callused skin.

Branches plucked at his clothes
like an anxious wife,
or slapped him away
like an angry one.
He thought he could feel
the hot breath
of hunting dogs.

He stumbled
through tall reeds, tore
at his own throat for breath.
On his knees, at bay
amid his brothers, he turned,

his chest hardening to lignin,
the laughter of women
in the thickets of his ears.

In the darkening corner of vision
a kingfisher's sharp blue flame.

vi A Superfluity of Nuns

What could Christ want
with so many wives?

Cloistered women
in their dark habits

of obedience, shut up
at night like hens in a run?

A sanctified harem of
shrouded flesh, pale

as loaves of new-risen
bread, the mute tongues

of their patellae worn flat.
Ranks and rows of women

the Armada of God,
wimples set like spinnakers

tacking bravely across the storm.

vii **An Observance of Hermits**

He'd never been good at people –
their hands were too big, and their teeth gleamed.

And their eyes, the clamour of them, staring at him
made his skull ring with voices, telling lies.
Someone was always watching.

Eight months since it was cut, his hair
as long and matted as the eremites',
his patron saints – Benedict, Anthony.

He speaks their names lovingly, as
brick by brick, he walls himself in

humming hymns as the candle flickers
and air and darkness thicken in his throat.

Beside him, voices are blessing his knife.
He's going to put out God's eyes.

viii **An Impertinence of Pedlars**

They have surrounded the house.
All day long, door-to-door salesmen
have brought their polished toe-caps
and polyester-gabardine trouser legs
to my front door.

They've rapped their shiny knuckles
in a percussive fugue – tympanic
booming, snare-like patter-tatting.

Some knocked three times or more,
some knocked twice
and then pretended to leave
to lure me into the hallway

but I am not deceived.

They are out there, clustered
like rabbits in the Mackenzie Country,
lounging by the lilac, swapping stories
about the-sale-that-got-away
and the ones that didn't

comparing the length
of their sales pitches.

They're taking turns
to stroll up and peer
through the kitchen window.

I don't know
how long I can hold out -
someone's rustling
through the potted lemon.

ix **A Host of Sparrows**

Observe the sparrows
             who cluster in drabs
and treat people as mobile dessert bars.
The sparrows who haunt our picnic tables

and wrestle with pigeons for crumbs and crusts,
who hop like beans in a frying pan,
one eye always perky for cats.

Study the sparrows
             who nest among downspouts,
in drainpipes, in ragged holes in the hedges,
who flutter and scuffle at traffic lights

snatching fag ends and chips
and their own wing tips
out from under huge wheels.

Consider the sparrows
             who've left behind wilderness
shifted to cities and married their cousins.
Moved in. Moved up. Made a niche.

x A Murder of Crows

For your widowhood –

a crow carved from obsidian,
from oilstone, from jet,
from the roof-beam
of your mother's house,
gutted by fire

> *In the first pass of the squeegee*
> *a flurry of dark wings*
> *reflected in the attic window –*
>
> *the window cleaner started.*
> *Just a crow, settling*
> *on the powerlines behind him.*

a crow with a cowl of anger,
feet burning with phosphate paste,
half-fledged

> *He'd shot crows as a boy –*
> *target practice, the birds deep*
> *in the guts of of a dying beast.*
>
> *In the second pass*
> *the darkness had multiplied –*
> *four more crows, motionless*
> *as though they'd grown there.*

a crow with an iron beak,
clattering in the ribs of something
that, whatever it *was*, now
is meat

> The wires were thick with them now,
> hunched like grief against the sky.

a crow to teach you: *lack*
a crow to teach you: *reave*
a crow to teach you: *reap*

> Backside against the brickwork
> he flapped the chamois at them –
> one or two fluttered away. Lazy.
> He hurled the squeegee,

a crow to show you
that a corvid's breastbone
is the keel of a longship,
cleaving the air

> and felt the ladder shift.

xi **A Bouquet of Pheasants**

When they mate, the rustling feathers
sound like taffeta –

a woman in a ball gown
fled into the garden to weep,

skirts bunched in her hands, a bruise
darkening the bare skin of her shoulder.

Wait. Her sobbing will soften into the breath
of night-scented stock –

the only sound left in all the wide night
is made by the pheasants stirring.

xii **A Skein of Geese**

He came to collect the last of his things
and she could see past him
someone else in the new car, waiting,
long fingers drumming on the door.

She lifted her heavy face
to stare instead at the sky, her body
echoing with his footsteps

until the door slammed
and they purred away into a distance
that made her dizzy and filled her ears
with the noise of rushing wings,

darkness against the clouds
became wild geese flying south,
the last threads of summer
unravelling behind them.

Ilkley

Past the vase
and the gaggle of stone houses

five white geese
cross a triangle of grass,
the last rocking back
and opening its wings

like the old man
emerging behind them,
stretching his arms
and slapping his wish-bone chest.

Nothing of my life is visible here –
blink twice, and I'll vanish.

Drowning

So, that's the ending;
two people
and an ocean of double bed

I will enter you
like water

our words were jagged
and the pillows salty
- I ached, he bled -

breathe me in, drown
in me

when I lift my head
a stretch of unmarked sand
waits for my footsteps

I will enter you
like water

for the word
to set my feet irrevocably
on that new shore

like water.

Stellaria Epithalamion

Today is your bridal, your wedding day.

I'm in the garden, pulling up
hanks of chickweed.

The flowers twinkle
like spatters of rain on the spade-shaped leaves,
and seeds speckle my hands.

Just yesterday we had supper together; complete
with the lecture you couldn't help giving
about chickweed - *stellaria media* - and others,
neglected but useful, once common as lettuce.
Come on, you said, *We'll make a salad of them!*
laughing our way through the garden at dusk
the colander filling with chickweed, purslane,
dandelion, sorrel - a dozen textures of green.

Candlelight, wine, hunks of fresh bread
and our vagabond salad. You smiled,
cupped my face in your hands
and kissed me ...

and today is your wedding day.
I'm weeding the garden, ripping out handfuls of
        chickweed,
and burning them.

What Comes After

To be married is to sit at the table each evening,
to take turns to put out the rubbish.
One washes up while the other dries.
Because you are married, you find
shirts perfectly ironed
and three good meals a day
cooked and politely eaten.

Slippers and spinning wheels
gather cobwebs in corners,
red cloaks are used for table cloths
and woodsmen commute
half an hour each day to work in an office.
The knock on the door is a Man
from the Council,
and what happens to little girls
alone in the woods
is far, far worse than wolves.

So collect the porridge bowls to wash up.
Tell yourself again; the sound of the front door
closing behind him each morning is nothing
like the clang of the witch's oven.

Canticle of the Harvest

The potatoes will yield fat fingers
of starchy goodness.
We will swaddle them
in hessian sacks
like babies in a maternity ward.

The carrots will bide
their amber time,
comfortable in the earth
like a thumb in the mouth
of a three-year-old child.

The clasped palms of garlic
will be lifted and dried,
plaited together in a fragrant stole.

*And the corn, drying
for next year's seed?*

– ah, the corn.
Peel back husks like lips,
and the kernels chatter
and grin like the teeth
of peat-bog dead.

The Uses of Linen

Two ells of fine-count linen,
this wedding veil, this shroud.

In the evenings of his absence
I sit, I set with my needle

such tiny stitches, such
delicate wounds

in the slub of linen,
the ghosting of skin.

My needle is a darting bird,

mute against the roar
of this empty room.

I tell myself; soon the traveller
will watch from this window

the sun rise and sail without him.

Each stitch I set, each
crewel knot is a promise

that I will keep and he
will break, before he returns to me.

The Willow

When my man first brought me here
this window framed the willow tree,
sunlight stinted through its grey fingers –
even in summer this room was cold.

And everyone knows about willow roots,
how the blind white tips swarm into pipes.
They parched the trees I planted,
riddled my garden, my bed.

Each evening he'd go to the willow,
lean back against a trunk
that seemed to curve toward his body.
He took his grief there when his mother died.

When he died, I took the axe myself,
exulted in the heft and swing, the bite
of blade into limb,
the shriek of timber falling.

There is light now, sunlight.
Spring steps over the windowsill.

Iphigenia

What man betrays his daughter
to fill out the slack in his sails?

A bloke in the pub told him she was the cause
and the cure for the halcyon summer.

She dressed for celebration,
her mother's pearls at her throat,

twelve-year-old girl
in borrowed high heels.

- Sit with me, daughter.

Her fingers were sticky with oyster sauce,
he refilled her glass with wine.

- Come with me, daughter,

the hand on her shoulder a tether,
the hand on her breast a knife.

The storytellers lied –

there was no divine intervention.
Her ragged breath filled their sails.

The Damaged

Against a backdrop of lost Atlantis
they come, one after the other
in chariots of steel and webbing –
a beautiful boy with an emptied face,
a gaunt girl with a thick black mane
whose hands beat and beat the air, escaping,
a child with a sharp crooked spine,
limbs tangled like mangrove roots.

Grown men lift them from their chairs,
bear them into the pool, light
as petals in their arms – the damaged
children with lotus faces, who slip free
of their bodies into the water, and blossom.

I Wish You Angels –

riding up and down
and up in elevators
crowding around your
computer screen
emailing God
in the lunch break.

Angels scalding
their tongues tasting
coffee, constrained
to *'drat'* and *'darn'*
and *'oooohhhh!'*
I wish you Angels staring

into department-store
windows, striking up
conversations with dress
shop dummies. I wish
you Angels with fishnet
stockings and misplaced

body piercings, two years
behind the trend. Angels
trying to follow cricket
or rugby, buffeting spectators
with jubilant wings.
I wish you Angels

drag-racing owls
at midnight, Angels
perched on traffic lights
drumming aimless feet
against the green,
I wish you Angels,

whistling.

Mrs Winslow's Deformed Left Ankle

hung over her shoe
like a stockinged haggis.

I used to be a dancer, she told me
when I dragged my eyes to her face.
Her hands flitted sideways, *a dancer ...*

she stepped forward *sur la pointe*
arching into an arabesque,
grizzled hair gleaming black
against a beaded satin headdress,
her stained woollen skirt
twitching into a tutu;

                      Odette
caught in a shaft of sunlight
in the supermarket carpark.

A car honked. She dropped her hands
to her sides, nodded, hobbled away,
pendulous with her shopping bags
and her swan's foot.

Gabriel

A boy with hair like sand in the rain,
cropped to cup the bones
of his skull as closely as the priest

who, with three palmfuls of water,
washed him from his mother's body,
into the kingdom of his name.

Ebb

The estuary is mumbling to itself.
Someone's labrador bounds past, barking,
a wet-feather smell ebbing into salt and spray.
Your arms prickle with goosebumps, as the easterly
wraps our skirts hobble-tight around bare legs
and our footprints bloom and fade in wet sand.

I lose your voice to the breakers, turn,
catch you smiling – I will remember this –
your face tilted against the grey sea dusk,
and beyond the dunes
the defiant purple of thistles.

Breaking Up

The left index finger was first. It fell without
    warning, smashing
on the floor between us. Tiny faults
ran up the palm, past the wrist. A cobwebbing
    of weakness,
the whole left arm misted in a glove of silk lace.

You reached out, barely flinched when the skin
    blackened at your touch,
crumbled into dust leaving arm bones naked. The
    torso cracked
like an ancient glaze, flesh peeling off in flakes and
    slivers and sheets,
dissolving in the twin gusts of our breathing.

From the hands the tiny bones - carpals,
    phalanges - dropped
like pins, a rain of bones, pattering
until all that was left of us was a rib cage, propped
    up
like a recipe book, an empty box, a sprung trap,

and all you said as you turned away
was that it proved I'd never really loved you.

The Lake

How casually waves
slap the shore,

leave it shocked,
open mouthed
and silent.

The pier braced
against the lake

is the spine
of a woman,
the booted feet

of the fisherman
on her shoulder-blades,

lures of bright metal
glittering like promises
through weed and rocks.

*May the wind change
to the south,*

*snag his line
around branches
and submerged roots,*

*pale fingers tangled
in deep water*

he'd said:
'It could swallow me.
I would sink and sink

and never touch
the heart of this lake ...'

Night Rain

Outside in the dark
a cow is bellowing for the calf
that was bundled into a trailer,
and taken away.

In another country
you're getting ready for bed,
wallet and keys flung down
in a heap on the dresser,
like children
suddenly tired of games.

I close the window
against the steady rain.
All night the cow will
pace the fenceline

making the sounds
that I cannot,
being human, and adult,
and to blame.

Curly Hill Road

Walking back to an empty house
through the dusk of that first summer,
I watched pipistrelles hunting

their high, thin calls like the chink
of ice-glazed tinsel

as they flung themselves after moths,
pivoting midair
on the point of an elbow

as though skin could stretch indefinitely,
as though bones never snapped.

Parable of the Drought

He got up from the narrow bed
and shaved off his beard,
rinsing his face and the razor
with a last mugful of fresh water.
He dressed, and waited
for sunlight through the window
to wake the boy.

They walked all morning,
following the sun and the line
of fenceposts that shimmered west.
He looked only once at the sky,
shading his eyes
when a black cockatoo flew overhead.

When they came to broken country
the bloodwood and gidgee
sucked the shade back into themselves.
Heat smashed against the gibbers.

He kissed the boy's forehead
and held his skinny shoulders,
breathing his scent of smoke and dust and sweat
and a sweetness
that for a moment could have been his wife.
He slid his fingers into the boy's hair
- *just like a wether,* he thought, *just like a ewe* -

He watched until the boy's eyes
lost their brilliance – the same brittle blue
as the sky that even now
refuses to cloud.

Notes

In the voices of tarapunga: 'tarapunga' is the Maori name for *Larus novaehollandiae*, the Red-billed Seagull. In much Maori mythology they are believed to embody the spirits of the ancestors.

Skeleton: 'skeleton' sledding is a winter sport similar to luge. The main difference between skeleton and luge is the competitor's position on the sled – prone rather than supine, head first rather than feet first. Also known as 'Cresta', after the Cresta Run.

The Orange Tree: 'satinbird' is the common name for *Ptilonorhynchus Violaceus*, the Satin Bowerbird. Known for its love of the colour blue.

'Shield bugs', *Biprorulus bibax*, are a common pest in citrus orchards in much of New South Wales. When disturbed the bugs squirt a foul-smelling fluid that can burn skin and eyes.

Bede's Sparrow: 'cunjevoi' (*Alocasia brisbanensis*) is a lily-like plant that occurs in rainforests from north-east NSW to north Queensland, and into south-east Asia. It has large, heart-shaped, dark green leaves, fragrant yellow flowers and highly toxic red berries.

Phlogiston: 'phlogiston' was the substance once believed to be the flammable component of all combustible materials. From the Greek *phlogistos*, meaning 'flammable'.

Venery: the poems in this sequence are all based on collective noun phrases from 'The Book of St Albans', generally attributed to a Dame Julianna Barnes (or Berners, or Bernes). Printed in 1486, it contained instruction on the gentlemanly arts of Hunting, Hawking and Heraldry, and included lists of the correct collective nouns for a wide variety of animals and people. It is believed that most of these collective nouns were invented by Dame Julianna.

A Knot of Toads: the cane toad (*Bufo marinus*) was introduced into Australia to control beetles in the cane fields of Queensland. One of the worst environmental disasters in Australian history, they have spread across most of Queensland and the Northern Territory, and into increasingly large areas of New South Wales. They compete with (and prey on) most native amphibians, and are themselves extremely toxic at all stages of their lives. They have no known natural predators.

An Impertinence of Pedlars: 'the Mackenzie Country' is a high inland plateau beneath the Southern Alps in the central South Island of New Zealand. Introduced rabbits have become a catastrophic problem, leading in 1997 to a group of farmers smuggling in vials of rabbit-calicivirus from Australia. The illegal release of the virus had only a limited effect.

Acknowledgements

Versions of some of these poems have appeared in the following publications:

Acumen, Agenda, Barnwood Poetry Magazine, Best Australian Poems 2005, Big Sky, Cordite, Envoi, Glottis, He drew down blue from the sky to make a river (2004 Arvon Competition Anthology), *Imago, The Interpreter's House, Iota, JAAM, LiNQ, Magma, New Poetries IV, Poetry New Zealand, Poetry Wales, The Press, A Savage Gathering, Seam, Smiths Knoll, Smoke, Southerly, Sub Tropics, Takahe, Tirra Lirra, The Unbelievable Lightness of Eggs.*

The author also wishes to thank Gillian Clarke, Sheenagh Pugh and Tony Curtis at the University of Glamorgan; and Helen Bascand, James Norcliffe, David Howard and Airing Cupboard Women Poets for their support.